THE WAY TO DISCIPLESHIP

Thinking Well About the Kingdom of God

Curtis L. Ferrell

CLF Ministries

To
Cheryl,
Kaitie, Nick, Emily,
Mom and Dad

and
Dr. Michael S. Heiser

As egg-headed as it may sound,
our basic problem is our theology.

DALLAS WILLARD

CONTENTS

PREFACE

This book was birthed during my final course at Redemption Seminary as I was completing my Master of Arts in Biblical Studies, but the gestation period of the book spans most of my life.

I have witnessed Christian ministry leaders living with the chronic frustration of understanding God's commission to the church, but not seeing it become a reality in their congregations. A quick search of Amazon reveals over 30,000 books on discipleship. There are over 10,000 discipleship studies. Churches regularly schedule discipleship classes and develop discipleship programs, but the fruit of healthy growing disciples who make disciples is frustratingly elusive.

Nearly every congregation will say that the Great Commission is one of its priorities, and yet successful discipleship is almost nonexistent in North America. In my studies it has become clear that our struggle with effective discipleship is not due to a lack of will on God's behalf, nor is it due to an unwillingness on behalf of the church. Neither can a lack of authority or spiritual power be to blame for the ongoing struggle between "what is" and "what should be." I am convinced that at the root of the struggle is a lack of clarity in what we believe.

My final project was designed to help ministry leaders recognize the need for corrective action and to provide a roadmap for making those corrections. This book is the product of those efforts.

Curt Ferrell
March 2024

FOREWORD BY
JEANNETTE FLYNN

I grew up on a large working farm with three brothers. My great-grandparents farmed their whole lives, my grandparents were farmers, and my parents farmed. That meant all four of us children learned to farm. Up early, managing the chores with all the animals. Driving tractors before our feet touched the pedals. Bucking bales of hay up to the wagon and then storing them in the loft of the barn. Filling the silos with grain that was harvested. Well, you get the picture.

Now let me tell you, not one of my brothers nor myself farm today – in any measure! In fact, when we get together for sibling reunions, we sit around and tell, what I call, "sanitized stories" about growing up on the farm. We reminisce about the fun we had. The freedom to roam like 'free range kids.' Jumping from haylofts. Catching cows to try and ride them, and hypnotizing the poor chickens. We laugh, we remember, and with each retelling, there is less and less of what real farming was and is about. We tell "sanitized" memories of the good old days!

I'm afraid that far too often we have done the same thing in our churches and with our faith. We love to sing the songs we love and sit in the spot that we've always sat in. We rehearse our "Amen!" and shake our heads about "those" wicked people, then look heavenward while affirming we love Jesus. The problem is we have not been thoughtful and intentional about being discipled, or discipling others. We have a surface faith that isn't prepared to authentically explain how a "loving God could allow my child to die," or how to answer a person who says, "Well, as long as they are sincere about believing in their God, aren't we all going to the same place?" We have no idea how to address the far left or the radical right! Don't we just need to condemn sinners, and sing our hymns, and wait for the chariot to pick us up and deliver us at the pearly gates?

Well, that is not at all what Jesus intended for those who have accepted Him as Lord and Savior. He identified them as Kingdom Citizens! Disciples in the Kingdom of God, who are entrusted as keepers of the new covenant and commissioned to go and share the gospel with their whole world. Followers who, having studied and prepared as workers, are not ashamed and, correctly handle the word of truth. (2 Timothy 2:15). Disciples who allow scripture to rebuke, correct, and train them in righteousness so that they are thoroughly equipped for every good work. (2 Timothy 3:16 – 17).

Statistics today reveal a very small percentage of churches are actively engaged in strategically creating a culture where they invest in "reproducing discipleship." We've "sanitized" discipleship! We've said people are too busy and rationalize that "theology divides us anyway. At best, we may offer classes that welcome folks to our churches and introduce them to our staff and church. Or perhaps we offer a class about basic beliefs we have in our church. But, we are still a long way off from authentically, and intentionally, discipling believers to be grounded in their faith; disciples who fully understand why they believe what they believe, and that they are commissioned to make disciples who make disciples! That, my friends, is the kind of discipleship that this manual offers help for.

Rev. Curtis Ferrell sounds a clear call for the church to restore biblically sound discipleship at every level and in all areas of ministry. He offers seven key points of understanding and discipleship that need to be addressed in the church today so that the church can fulfill her God-appointed mission. Ferrell guides us into understanding the Kingdom of God, here on earth, as it is lived out by Kingdom citizens who know the King. Kingdom citizens who prepare themselves to be equipped and who are ready to carry out the mission of reaching a lost and broken world.

If you are pastoring or teaching and feel the pressure and challenge of helping those you serve to live the message of Jesus Christ – living as though it was actually true and really mattered for our world today – then *The Way to Discipleship: Thinking Well About the Kingdom of God* is a book you will not only read but use as a discipleship tool to effectively equip others.

We have a choice to make. We can continue to tell our "sanitized" testimonies, raise our hands when we sing, look radiant when talking about how much we love Jesus, and continue to die! Or we can answer the challenge Rev. Ferrell is sounding and begin to thoughtfully develop, plan, and prepare methods of discipleship that change the culture; authentic biblical discipleship that produces a culture where we know who we are in Christ and what His call on our life means. And if we step into the power of Holy Spirit-filled discipleship, we will begin to live as He designed and commissioned us to live! We will grow as His disciples, fully equipped so that even the gates of hell won't prevail against us.

The world is watching! It has been waiting for a long time for us to live out what the word of God calls us to. We have a decision to make. Shall we continue with our sanitized versions, rehearsing the good old days? Or, shall we take hold of the scripture and let the scripture take hold of us, as we follow our Lord and Savior on His mission to rescue the lost and heal the broken?

> *I call heaven and earth to witness against you today, that I have set before you life and death, blessing and curse. Therefore choose life, that you and your offspring may live, loving the LORD your God, obeying his voice and holding fast to him, for he is your life and length of days, that you may dwell in the land that the LORD swore to your*

fathers, to Abraham, to Isaac, and to Jacob, to give them.
(Deuteronomy 30:19-20)

Rev. Jeannette Flynn

Church of God Ministries

FOREWORD BY
JERRY INGALLS

The imagery is clear, and the message is strong! *The Way to Discipleship: Thinking Well About the Kingdom of God* is a must-read for all who love Jesus and desire to see His body return to the Founder's intent. I've known author Curt Ferrell for years as a trusted friend, prayer partner, and fellow student of the Word. Curt is a pastor, but, more importantly, he is a long-time, committed disciple of Jesus. He knows the heart of God and loves to lead people into His presence through worship leadership and biblical preaching. Over the last decade, I have watched Curt go through a course correction in his life and ministry, as the Lord opened his eyes to the importance and urgency of Christian discipleship as the engine of the Church. He has learned that discipleship is not a program or a curriculum; it's the very essence of who we are and why we exist. Curt is now sharing with you the journey the Lord took him on first.

This book was on time for me, as I trust that it will be for you, because the time is now for the Church to make the necessary course corrections to put first things first in every aspect of what we do. While this material was developed in an academic setting, it is designed to be accessible for the Church, from the most experienced pastor in the pulpit to the newest convert in the pew. I want to emphasize to you that this is not a program or curriculum; this is a strategic opportunity to be transformed through the renewing of your mind. I inform you ahead of time that this book will challenge your presuppositions about so much of what you assume you already know. It will do so in the best of ways, as Curt guides you on a biblical journey from Genesis to Revelation into the heart of God, the purpose of His creation, why He made people as Image Bearers, why He sent His son Jesus Christ, the call upon the Church as God's Plan A, and to what end God desires for His Kingdom to come on Earth as it is in Heaven.

This book may fill in some of the gaps in your understanding of the Gospel, answer some of those nagging questions that have gone unanswered for so many years, or straight up rock your boat! If you are willing and ready to make the necessary course corrections to align your life, and your local church's ministry, with Jesus' call to discipleship, then don't delay any longer. Start reading today and take the first step on your journey into being an active participant in the greatest story ever told. Remember, a ship that is set in dry dock can't be steered. Bon voyage!

Dr. Jerry D. Ingalls

Lead Pastor, First Baptist Church, New Castle, IN

BEFORE YOU READ
THIS BOOK

In the space below and on the next page, answer these questions *BEFORE YOU READ THIS BOOK*:

1.　　How do you determine whether ministry is effective?

2.　　What is discipleship?

3.　　What is the Great Commission?

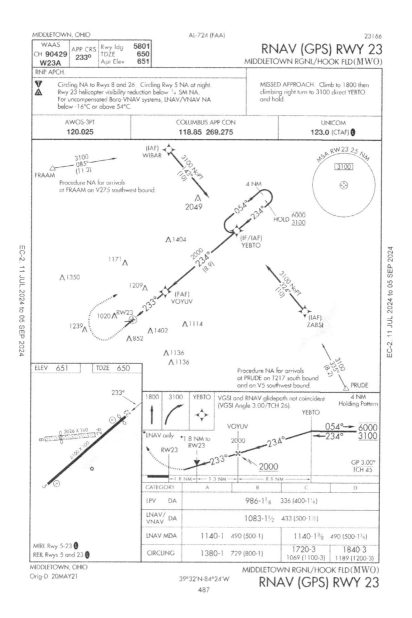

THE PROBLEM

T he mission couldn't be any clearer. Make disciples (Matthew 28:18-20; 2 Timothy 2:2; 2 Timothy 3:16-17; Colossians 1:28-29). The church has embraced the mission and even given it a special name – The Great Commission. After the resurrection, Jesus was given all authority in heaven and earth, including authority over the mission. The Holy Spirit was given to the church to accomplish the will of God on earth as it is in heaven. And yet, there is a problem as noted in a recent study.

A 2020 study of churches in the United States found that fewer than five percent of churches have a "reproducing disciple-making culture."[1] Many Protestant pastors claim to have effective disciple-making activities but cannot point to any significant spiritual impact made by these activities.[2] Unfortunately, nearly thirty percent of congregations have a negative impact on disciple-making because they don't intentionally focus on helping others make disciples or grow in their relationship with Christ.[3]

Christian philosopher and theologian Dallas Willard observed that in the church there is an even deeper problem. One "is not required to be ... a disciple in order to become a Christian, and one may remain a Christian without any signs of progress toward, or in, discipleship."[4] "We have multitudes of professing Christians who well may be ready to die but obviously are not ready to live, and can hardly get along with themselves, much less with others."[5]

The mission is clear. The church has embraced the mission. Christ has given the church authority (Matthew 28:18-20; Luke 10:19; Genesis 1:26-28) and the power (Acts 1:8) to accomplish the mission. However, nearly all Christians today assume that we can 'be "Christians" forever and never become disciples.'[6] In practice, discipleship has become an optional "add-on" for extra credit in our pursuit of Christ. So where is the disconnect?

I believe the disconnect is due to a series of slight but significant misunderstandings of key biblical concepts, including the Great Commission. A one-degree error in navigation can, over time, be disastrous. In the physical world, navigators have found a way to avoid disaster.

In a long journey by plane, there are several *"waypoints"* designated by GPS that mark what amounts to intersections in imaginary highways in the sky. At each of these waypoints, pilots, or more commonly computers, make slight course corrections to keep the plane headed in the right direction. In a long journey, say across a continent or ocean, a one-degree error could result in being miles from your intended destination. A one-degree error in a journey to the moon could prove deadly. If discipleship is the church's moonshot, we are headed for deep space and a cold, dark future.

Fortunately, making a series of minor course corrections at seven waypoints in our journey could put us back on the path toward our intended destination. As presented here, *The Way to Discipleship: Thinking Well About the Kingdom of God* provides ministry leaders with the biblical foundation to accurately define discipleship and to design and evaluate whether their ministries are in alignment with that definition.

The Way to Discipleship: Thinking Well About the Kingdom of God helps ministry leaders utilize scripture to deconstruct a faulty image of discipleship, and then, using small but significant one-degree course corrections, reconstruct a biblically defined vision of what discipleship looks like in their ministry context.

You may be tempted to get to the destination quicker and bypass one or more of these waypoints, but each course correction is crucial to safely arriving at our destination. Like any flight, much of our journey will be through blue skies. However, we may occasionally encounter turbulence when the warm air of scripture rises over the cooler air of tradition.

Our Compass – Seek First the Kingdom of God

And since GPS only works for a physical journey, we will need a spiritual compass for making each of these one-degree course corrections. Our compass is found in Matthew 6:33 (ESV): "Seek first the *kingdom of God* ..." If we are seeking the Kingdom of God first, we won't have to be anxious about our discipleship efforts. We will be back on course toward an exciting new country!

Imagine a land where gift-based ministry surpasses program-based ministry. Picture discipleship that not only imparts knowledge about the Kingdom of God but also transforms passions and desires. Envision a world where disciples will not only have a solid Scriptural foundation but there will also be a revolution in their habits and responses to challenging situations. In this world ministry leaders could be freed from administrative tasks, enabling them to invest more time in long-term, intentional relationships that produce disciples who make more disciples.

This could be the destination for your ministry if you allow your compass and *The Way to Discipleship: Thinking Well About the Kingdom of God* to pilot you through these minor course corrections. If you are ready to go, the gate is open, and you are free to board.

194

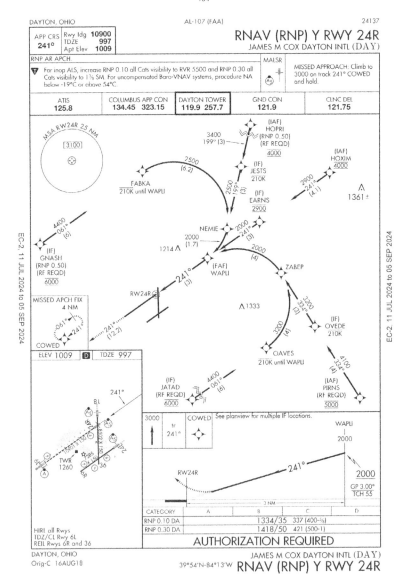

WAYPOINT 1 – THE INITIATION OF THE KINGDOM OF GOD

If We Don't Understand The Metanarrative, We Won't Understand The Vision, Mission, Purpose, Or Identity

What is a "metanarrative?" A metanarrative is an all-encompassing, overarching foundational story. There are hundreds of short stories, or narratives, in scripture, but there is one metanarrative, an overarching story, that begins in Genesis 1 and continues through the end of Revelation.

As we map out our disciple-making journey, using our Kingdom of God compass, our first waypoint is identifying the overarching story of scripture. It's the story of the Kingdom of God.

A simple definition of the Kingdom of God is that his kingdom exists everywhere God's rule extends, AND his will is done. In the beginning, God's kingdom extended over the face of the deep when he said, "Let there be light!"

In the first three chapters of Genesis, we see God creating the world with intentionality. Let there be light. Let there be an expanse in the sky. Let the waters be gathered. Let the dry land appear. Let the earth sprout vegetation. Let there be the sun, moon, and stars. Let the waters swarm with living creatures. Let the sky be filled with birds. Let the earth bring forth living creatures. Let us make mankind in our image. God's will and reign extended over all creation. And it was very good.

And to the man and woman, God said, "Be fruitful, multiply, fill the earth, subdue it, and have dominion." In effect, God delegated stewardship authority to the man and woman to continue his reign and accomplish his will on earth. We'll expand on this more in the next section.

Every Sunday School student is familiar with what happens next – the fall, the separation from God, and the expulsion from the garden. The man and the woman disobeyed the will of God and handed authority over to the serpent.

God had designed and executed an intentional plan for creation, but now a few questions arise. Did that plan just evaporate after Genesis 3? Did the heart of God abandon his carefully thought-out plan? What was God's vision for creation?

Even in the moment of the fall in the garden, God had a plan for redemption (Genesis 3:15). In the fullness of time the seed of the woman would crush the serpent. And throughout the rest of scripture, we see this plan fleshed out in two ways.

First, creation and redemption are the two dominant themes of scripture[7] and they frequently appear side by side in the same passage (John 1:1-14; Ephesians 2:8-16; Hebrews 1:1-4; Psalm 8;

Mark 16:15-16; Acts 17:22-31; 2 Corinthians 4:6; 2 Corinthians 5:16-20; Galatians 6:14-15; Ephesians 1:3-10; Ephesians 3:7-12, Ephesians 4:17-24; Colossians 1:13-23; Colossians 3:5-11; Hebrews 2:5-9).

Secondly, we see in the heart of God the desire to make all things new – re-creation (Isaiah 65:17; Isaiah 66:22; Matthew 19:28; Acts 3:19-21; 2 Corinthians 5:17; James 1:17-18; 2 Peter 3:13; Revelation 21:1-5).

The redemption promised in the garden is not simply to deal with sin in the hearts of fallen humanity; the promised redemption is for all of creation that has endured the effects of the curse of sin. During Second Temple Judaism there was a growing belief, especially among the Pharisees, that the universe God had created was essentially good, but was marred by sin and depravity, and according to the prophets, there was coming an age when God would make all things new.[8]

Why is it important to believe that creation is good and that God is making all things new? Because the typical story we tell in the church today is that someday we will leave this corrupt earth and these corruptible bodies, and our spirits will live with God in heaven. This version of the story is told repeatedly in sermons about heaven, during eulogies at funerals, and in our favorite hymns. "I'll Fly Away," "When We All Get To Heaven," and even in "Amazing Grace"; *When we've been there ten thousand years, bright shining as the sun ...*

But if that is the case, we are faced with several unanswerable questions. Why do the scriptures promise we will receive new resurrected physical bodies? Why does scripture say there will be a new earth? And if all creation (including our bodies) is going to be discarded, is there any justification for stewardship of creation in this age?

This is the trap we fall into when we forget the overarching story of scripture.

The Kingdom of God was initiated during creation. God repeatedly declared creation "good." The fall in the garden brought corruption into creation, but God has promised redemption and re-creation. He is making all things new. This is where we make our first one-degree course correction on the way to our destination of a disciple-making church.

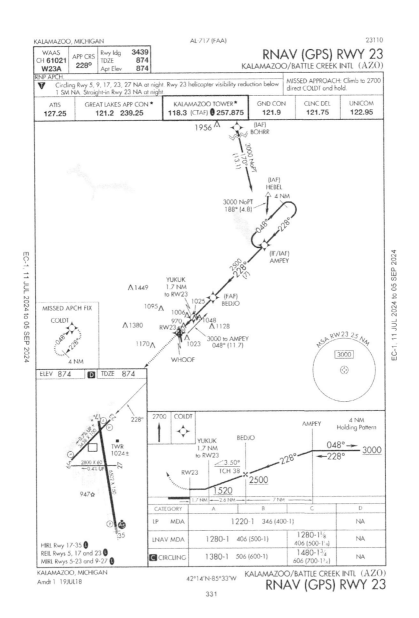

WAYPOINT 2 – STEWARDS OF THE KINGDOM OF GOD

We Must View Ourselves The Way God Views Us

T he second waypoint we encounter on our journey to a disciple-making church is understanding the purpose of humanity in the Kingdom of God, and specifically the purpose of God's people. Why did God create humans and what did he expect them to do? The answer to this question will shape our understanding of discipleship and is found when we take another look at creation.

Regardless of how Christians view the Creation accounts (there are at least five: the literal view[9], the literary framework view[10], the analogical days view[11], the evolutionary creationism view[12], and the identity accounts view[13]), there is at least one thing they all agree on. God did not instantaneously create a perfect, self-governing world. He created a world that required his action, in time, to make it good.

The earth was formless and void. Darkness was over the face of the deep. God hovered over the face of the waters. God said, "Let there be light." The first day. (Genesis 1:3-4)

God separated the waters above from the waters below and created the sky. The second day. (v.6-8)

God gathered the waters under the sky creating the land and sea. And it was good. God brought forth vegetation and seed-bearing plants. And it was good. The third day. (v.9-13)

God created the sun, moon, and stars. And it was good. The fourth day. (v.14-19)

God created the sea creatures and sky creatures. And it was good the fifth day. (v.20-23)

God created land creatures. And it was good. And God created humans to steward the earth. And it was very good. The sixth day. (v.24-31)

God who is eternal, who exists outside of time, intentionally created a world that required his action in time. He could have created a world that was instantly perfect and required no intervention on his part. He could just as easily have said, "Let there be the universe!" But God was intentional.

And in the middle of that sixth day God intentionally created humans with a purpose in mind.

26 Then God said, "Let us make man in our image, after our likeness. And let them have dominion over the fish of the sea and over the birds of the heavens and over the livestock and over all the earth and over every creeping thing that creeps on the earth."
27 So God created man in his own image,
   in the image of God he created him;
   male and female he created them.
28 And God blessed them. And God said to them, "Be fruitful and multiply and fill the earth and subdue it, and have dominion over

the fish of the sea and over the birds of the heavens and over every living thing that moves on the earth." (Genesis 1:26–28 ESV)

The purpose for humanity, given before God created them, is to act on God's behalf within Creation; to be God's stewards of the newly inaugurated Kingdom of God. God alone is Sovereign, and he commissioned humanity to steward his kingdom.

And this commission is reiterated and alluded to throughout the rest of scripture (Genesis 2:15; Genesis 9:1, 7; Genesis 16:10; Genesis 17:6-7; Genesis 22:16-18; Genesis 26:23-24; Genesis 28:1-4; Genesis 35:9-12; Genesis 41:50-52; Genesis 48:2-4; Exodus 1:7; Leviticus 26:9-13; Deuteronomy 7:12-14; Jeremiah 23:3-4; John 15:7-8; John 15:16).

There is another thread throughout scripture that highlights the stewardship and representative role of God's people (people who are in a right relationship with God), and that is being a kingdom of priests (Exodus 19:5-6; Deuteronomy 7:6-8; Isaiah 61:5-7; 1 Peter 2:9-10; Revelation 1:4-6; Revelation 5:9-10).

When Jesus was using parables to describe the Kingdom of God, he used the analogy of a man going on a journey and entrusting his property to his servants to steward on his behalf while he was gone (Matthew 25:14-30). Luke records Jesus giving a similar analogy in Luke 12:35-48, this time using the imagery of the stewards waiting for the groom to come home from the wedding feast. Interestingly, this story comes on the heels of Luke's version of our Kingdom of God compass, where Jesus then says, "Fear not, little flock, for it is your Father's good pleasure to give you the kingdom." (Luke 12:31-32)

As we will see later, the Great Commission can even be viewed as an extension of the role of God's people as stewards of creation and representatives of the Kingdom of God.

Why is it important to believe that every human was created as a steward of creation and a representative of the Kingdom of God?

Because it reminds us that there is no human who is purposeless; there are only people who don't know that God intentionally designed them to represent him in this world. But fallen human beings are incapable of fully representing God in the world. We needed someone who could remedy our fallenness once and for all, but that's a story for another waypoint.

God designed creation so that it needed his intervention, or intervention by his stewards. The Kingdom of God is depending on the stewardship of God's representatives. It's even groaning in anticipation for the revealing of God's children (Romans 8:19-20). This is our second waypoint as we make another one-degree course correction toward a disciple-making church.

18

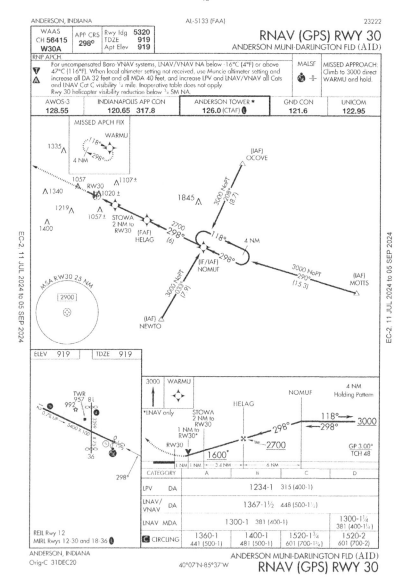

WAYPOINT 3 – THE GOSPEL OF THE KINGDOM OF GOD VS. OTHER GOSPELS

What Jesus Meant By "Gospel" Is Not What We Normally Mean

As we approach our third waypoint, we may encounter a little turbulence, so buckle up. I assure you that there are clear skies ahead.

I agree with Dallas Willard when he said, "As egg-headed as it may sound, our basic problem is our theology. The problem is our doctrine of salvation."[14] Our understanding of the word "*gospel*" is not so much wrong as it is limited.

When we use the term "*gospel*" we usually mean the events that happened on the cross and in the Resurrection. To most people, the significance of the gospel is that one can be delivered from sin so that they can live with Jesus in heaven. While this is not untrue, it differs significantly from what Jesus meant when he shared the good news (gospel).

The authors of the New Testament use the Greek word ευαγγελιον (*euangelion*) 134 times. For some reason, English translations usually use the phrase "good news" in Matthew, Mark, and Luke, but in the rest of the New Testament they tend to use the term "*gospel*" (interestingly, *euangelion* is never used in John). When *euangelion* is used in the first three Gospel accounts (except for Mark 1:1 where it is used as a title or descriptor of the book), it is the term used to describe the message of Christ ... before his death and resurrection.

The message that Christ preached was the message that the Kingdom of God was at hand (Mark 1:15). It was the message Jesus preached everywhere he went (Matthew 9:35; Matthew 11:5; Matthew 24:14; Luke 4:43; Luke 7:22; Luke 8:1; Luke 16:16; Luke 20:1). The Disciples preached the good news of the Kingdom of God (Luke 9:6). Jesus tells us what this good news is when he quotes from Isaiah in Luke 4:16-21. In none of these instances did Jesus or the disciples talk about his death and resurrection.

New Testament scholars note that in addition to the instances where Jesus uses the word *euangelion* there were several other times where he talked about the kingdom of God in parables and using other illustrations and metaphors.[15] But none of those included information about Christ's death and resurrection.

The message preached after the cross _of course_ includes his death and resurrection, which is how the good news of the Kingdom of God is realized. If Christ did not die and rise again, the Kingdom of God would have been lost forever in the wake of the fall in the garden. And the Apostle Paul says that our preaching would then be in vain as well as our very faith (1 Corinthians 15:13-14).

But Christ _did_ die for our sins and _did_ rise again on the third day. And being the new representative of the human race, the second Adam (1 Corinthians 15:42-49), Christ reclaimed the authority that the first man and woman lost in the fall, securing the eternal reality of the Kingdom of God.

Why is it important to understand that Jesus preached the gospel of the Kingdom of God? Because, according to Bill Hull and Ben Sobels, the most common version of the gospel preached in the developed world today is the forgiveness-only gospel.[16] In fact Hull has identified at least five different gospels that have been, and continue to be, preached in churches today:[17] the forgiveness-only gospel, the gospel of the left, the prosperity gospel, the consumer gospel, and the gospel of the right.

N.T. Wright says, "the movement that has long called itself 'evangelical' is in fact better labeled 'soterian'. That is, we have thought we were talking about 'the gospel' when in fact we were concentrating on 'salvation.'"[18] Dallas Willard observed, "'Gospels of Sin Management' presume a Christ with no serious work other than redeeming humankind. On the right, they foster 'vampire Christians,' who only want a little blood for their sins but nothing more to do with Jesus until heaven, when they have to associate with him. On the left, they foster the Phariseeism of a more or less brutal social self-righteousness.'[19] A.W. Tozer identified it as a modern day heresy, "the widely accepted concept that we humans can choose to accept Christ only because we need him as Savior and that we have the right to postpone our obedience to him as Lord as long as we want to! … Salvation apart from obedience is unknown in the sacred Scriptures."[20]

We must preach the gospel of the Kingdom of God, purchased, and secured by Christ's sacrifice on the cross, who was validated by the resurrection (Romans 1:4). And we must preach it so consistently that when we say the word "*gospel*" no one can misunderstand it to mean saying a magic prayer that purchases a ticket to heaven.[21]

Until there is a common understanding that the gospel means "the kingdom of God is at hand because of what Christ did on the cross and is revealed in the power of the resurrection," our third course correction might include using the phrase "the gospel of the Kingdom of God" instead of using the truncated and misunderstood term "gospel."

268

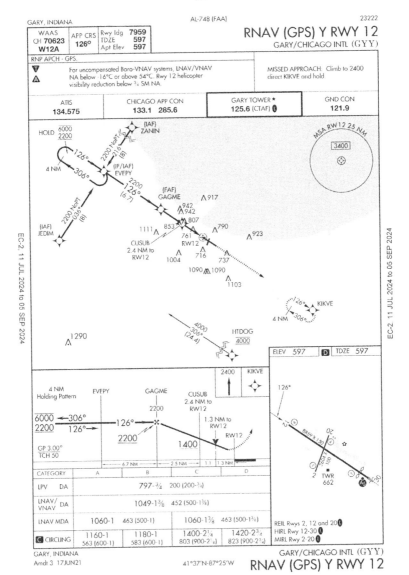

WAYPOINT 4 – THE RECONCILIATION OF THE STEWARDS OF THE KINGDOM OF GOD

Humans Are Incapable of Stewarding Without Reconciliation

Now that the skies have cleared a bit, we come to our fourth waypoint on the way to a disciple-making church. We have made one-degree corrections at the waypoints of Creation, Stewardship, and the Gospel, and can now deal with Salvation.

Why did humans need reconciliation with God? Typically, we answer, "Because all have sinned and fallen short of the glory of God" (Romans 3:23). But that's asking the question with the humans being the center of our perspective. What if we asked the question from the perspective of our compass verse, "Seek first the Kingdom of God?"

Why was it important *to the Kingdom of God* that Christ accomplished his Mission to bring about the reconciliation of humanity with God? To find the answer, we need to ask a few more questions.

In Romans 5:10-11 we see that, "while we were enemies we were reconciled to God by the death of his Son." This begs the question: if we have been reconciled (καταλλάσσω, *katallassō*) to God through Christ, meaning that we were restored to a previously broken relationship or position, where and when was that relationship broken? Wasn't that in the Garden?

But the fall in the garden happened *after* the Genesis Commission in Genesis 1:26-28. So, the next question is, was that first commission forever lost, never to be restored? Before we answer that question, let's look at another passage, Colossians 1:15-23 and pay special attention to verses 20 and 23:

> *15 [Christ] is the image of the invisible God, the firstborn of all creation. 16 For by him all things were created, in heaven and on earth, visible and invisible, whether thrones or dominions or rulers or authorities—all things were created through him and for him. 17 And he is before all things, and in him all things hold together. 18 And he is the head of the body, the church. He is the beginning, the firstborn from the dead, that in everything he might be preeminent. 19 For in him all the fullness of God was pleased to dwell, 20 and through him to reconcile to himself all things, whether on earth or in heaven, making peace by the blood of his cross.*
> *21 And you, who once were alienated and hostile in mind, doing evil deeds, 22 he has now reconciled in his body of flesh by his death, in order to present you holy and blameless and above reproach before him, 23 if indeed you continue in the faith, stable and steadfast, not shifting from the hope of the gospel that you heard, which has been proclaimed in all creation under heaven, and of which I, Paul, became a minister. (Colossians 1:15-23 ESV)*

This passage prompts a few more questions. Why was it necessary for Christ to "reconcile to himself all things?" Where was his relationship or position with "all things" broken? Wasn't God's relationship with all of Creation broken during the fall? If, as we saw at the last waypoint, "the gospel" is shorthand for the gospel of the Kingdom of God, what is the hope of the gospel of the Kingdom of God to all of creation?

At the second waypoint (Stewardship) we saw in Romans 8:19-20 that all creation is groaning in anticipation of the revealing of the children of God. But why does it groan for this? It's because the fall, recounted in Genesis 3, made it impossible for men and women to fully realize humanity's role as kingdom stewards. We needed reconciliation not only to deal with humanity's sin problem; we also needed reconciliation to restore our identity as stewards of creation and representatives of God in the world.

Why is it important to know and affirm that salvation was needed not only to deal with the sin problem, but also to restore men and women to their role as Stewards of creation and Representatives of God in the world? It's because as Stewards we have a job to do.

> *17 Therefore, if anyone is in Christ, he is a new creation. The old has passed away; behold, the new has come. 18 All this is from God, who through Christ reconciled us to himself and gave us the ministry of reconciliation; 19 that is, in Christ God was reconciling the world to himself, not counting their trespasses against them, and entrusting to us the message of reconciliation. 20 Therefore, we are ambassadors for Christ, God making his appeal through us. We implore you on behalf of Christ, be reconciled to God. 21 For our sake he made him to be sin who knew no sin, so that in him we might become the righteousness of God.* (2 Corinthians 5:17-21 ESV)

God has given his followers the ministry of reconciliation, entrusting to us the message of reconciliation. And reconciliation for humans means being restored to a right relationship with God which includes assuming the identity that God gave humans when he created them. N.T. Wright also notes that the term 'righteousness' "comes to mean, more or less, 'covenant membership', with all of the overtones of appropriate behavior."[22] When we are reconciled to God and our lives are transformed, we act in a way that reflects our role as Stewards of the Kingdom of God.

The commission given in Genesis 1:26-28 gave humanity their identity and purpose. Salvation, purchased by Christ's sacrifice on the cross, was needed to restore that identity and purpose in fallen men and women. The disciples saw the bodily resurrection of Christ as proof that the new age (when all things would be made new) had begun. In embracing these truths, we've made one more one-degree course correction toward a church whose business is making disciples who make disciples.

86

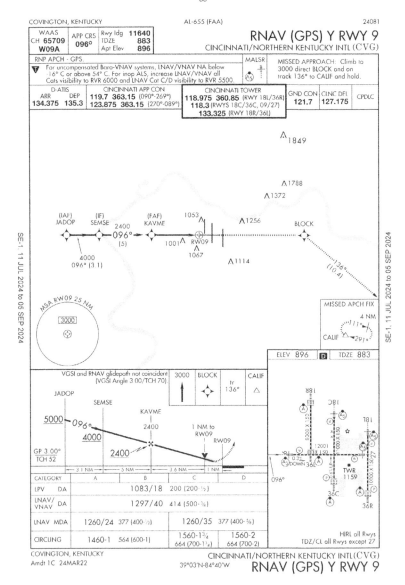

WAYPOINT 5 – THE RESTORATION OF THE STEWARDS OF THE KINGDOM OF GOD

We Must Be Restored As Stewards
To Accomplish God's Will

The fifth waypoint on our journey gets to the heart of our quest. What is the purpose of discipleship, and what does discipleship look like? Answering these questions will require a hard look at a traditional church perspective that's been around for nearly four hundred years.

In every generation, the church has tried different methods to disciple new believers. Some of these methods worked well, others not so much. In some generations, efforts at discipleship were very intense (i.e., John Wesley's Holy Club) and in other generations, discipleship efforts were almost non-existent (i.e., when citizens were required to become Christians and babies were baptized into church membership).

In 1642 the English Civil War broke out largely due to political, religious, and theological conflict.[23] In an effort to resolve the conflict, the Westminster Assembly was convened to bring some theological clarity and by 1647 it had produced the Westminster Shorter Catechism.[24]

The first question in the Westminster Shorter Catechism is:

> Question. 1. What is the chief end of man?
> Answer. Man's chief end is to glorify God, and to enjoy him forever.[25]

For nearly four hundred years this has been the position of the protestant church. But is it true? Look at *Ecclesiastes 12:13-14 (ESV):*

> *13 The end of the matter; all has been heard. Fear God and keep his commandments, for this is the whole duty of man. 14 For God will bring every deed into judgment, with every secret thing, whether good or evil.*

My contention is that "to glorify God, and to enjoy him forever" is a *byproduct* of the chief end of man, NOT the purpose of man. The purpose of mankind is to revere God and keep his commands, and the byproduct of doing that will result in us glorifying God and enjoying him forever.

If our purpose is to steward God's creation and be his representatives on earth, it seems that instead of "enjoying God and giving him glory," we would be better served by revering God and keeping his commands.

This one well-meaning creed may have done more to undermine a clear understanding of discipleship in the church than anything else. And if we revere God and keep his commands, what will appear on the horizon? Let's let scripture suggest a few things.

4 "Hear, O Israel: The LORD our God, the LORD is one. 5 You shall love the LORD your God with all your heart and with all your soul and with all your might. 6 And these words that I command you today shall be on your heart. 7 You shall teach them diligently to your children, and shall talk of them when you sit in your house, and when you walk by the way, and when you lie down, and when you rise. (Deuteronomy 6:4-7 ESV)

When we revere God and keep his commands, we will keep this command found in the *Shema*; "*You shall teach them diligently to your children, and shall talk of them when you sit in your house, and when you walk by the way, and when you lie down, and when you rise.*"

Shortly after the Westminster Shorter Catechism was created, English philosopher John Locke encouraged parents to embrace education for themselves because their primary duty was to educate their children.[26] One hundred years before that, Martin Luther developed his Small Catechism for parents to use in teaching their children the fundamentals of Christian faith.[27] What would it look like if the church developed tools for today's parents to teach their children about God?

But discipleship is more than the transfer of knowledge. Information must be transferred but that's only one side of the discipleship coin. True growth in disciples happen when they "live-out" the truths they discover, when information about Christ translates into living a Christ-like life. That means we must design discipleship paths that look more like apprenticeships; that make room for opportunities to live out learned truths.[28] True discipleship happens within relationships with other believers. The co-author of *DiscipleShift*, Bobby Harrington, says, "Discipleship is primarily about imitation over information, and it is through relationships that it most powerfully occurs."[29] And those relationships will encourage the disciples to move beyond imitation.

Discipleship is both orthodoxy (learning and believing truth about God) and orthopraxy (learning how to live-out that truth).

In sports we would say it's about learning the playbook AND running the drills. Harrington points out that "Jesus and the New Testament demonstrate that discipleship needs BOTH direction and relationship. Direction without relationship is a program approach to discipleship that says, 'Read this book. Take this class. Memorize these verses. Listen to these sermons. Memorize these answers. Follow these steps.' ... Conversely, relationship ... says, 'Let's just hang out together. Let's meet over coffee to talk. Let's enjoy one another.' ... Both guidance and relationship are essential. Biblical guidance and coaching, as defined by Jesus, and modeled by the apostles, is an intentional process, grounded in relationship."[30]

And those relationships need to be cross-generational according to Psalm 145:4-7 (ESV):

> 4 *One generation shall commend your works to another,*
> *and shall declare your mighty acts.*
> 5 *On the glorious splendor of your majesty,*
> *and on your wondrous works, I will meditate.*
> 6 *They shall speak of the might of your awesome deeds,*
> *and I will declare your greatness.*
> 7 *They shall pour forth the fame of your abundant goodness and*
> *shall sing aloud of your righteousness.*

These verses from John and Matthew suggest that disciples must continue Christ's work in the world:

> 4 *We must work the works of him who sent me while it is day; night is coming, when no one can work. 5 As long as I am in the world, I am the light of the world."* (John 9:4-5 ESV)

> 14 *"You are the light of the world. A city set on a hill cannot be hidden. 15 Nor do people light a lamp and put it under a basket, but on a stand, and it gives light to all in the house. 16 In the same way, let your light shine before others, so that they may see your good works and give glory to your Father who is in heaven.* (Matthew

5:14-16 ESV)

Notice the *"We"* at the beginning of John 9:4. We <u>must</u> be doing the works that God created specifically for us.

> *For we are his workmanship, created in Christ Jesus for good works, which God prepared beforehand, that we should walk in them.* (Ephesians 2:10 ESV)

One more thing to notice from scripture is found in Jesus's farewell prayer in *John 17:3-4 (ESV):*

> *3 "And this is eternal life, that they know you, the only true God, and Jesus Christ whom you have sent. 4 I glorified you on earth, having accomplished the work that you gave me to do."*

Jesus is claiming, before he went to the cross, that he had completed his work. Jim Putman, the other co-author of *DiscipleShift* notes, "As believers we know that His [Christ's] primary purpose for coming to earth was to pay for the sins of all who would accept His grace through faith. The Cross is clearly central to His mission. However, this passage reveals something else. Jesus is praying to the Father before the Crucifixion and the Resurrection. He says here that He has completed something. Completed what? I believe He was talking about having completed the training of His twelve disciples. He was ready to release them into the world to make disciples themselves."[31]

Why is it important to believe that Christ restores us to our role as stewards of the Kingdom of God? Because as we saw at our Gospel waypoint, if we focus on a forgiveness-only gospel and ignore the Kingdom of God gospel then discipleship gets framed as "preparing people for heaven."

Discipleship is not about making Christians fit for eternal life. We must see discipleship as equipping people to accomplish their Genesis Commission mandate. Discipleship is about equipping people to be God's representatives and stewards in this life as we advance the Kingdom of God.

Dallas Willard observes, "The most despicable as well as the most admirable of persons have had a spiritual formation. Their spirits or hearts have been formed. We all become a certain kind of person, gain a specific character, and that is the outcome of a process of spiritual formation understood in general human terms."[32] That is why Christian discipleship is necessary. We have all been "formed" spiritually, whether for good or bad. Discipleship is needed to form us into the image of the second Adam, so that we can be stewards of the Kingdom of God and representatives of God in the world.

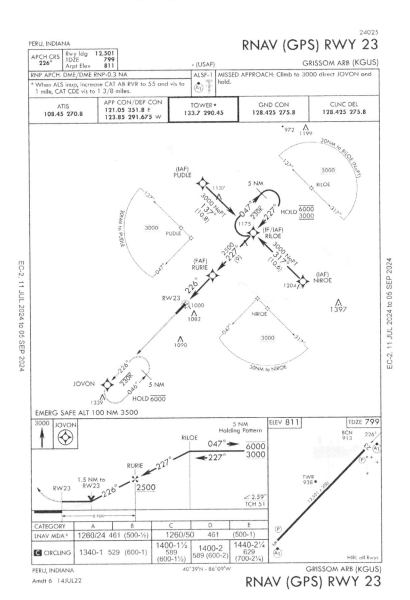

WAYPOINT 6 – THE MISSION OF THE STEWARDS OF THE KINGDOM OF GOD

It's An Every-Person, Everyday Mission
– Not Just To The Third World

W
e have one more waypoint before we begin our final approach toward a disciple-making church: The Great Commission. What is the Great Commission?

Try this exercise before we look at scripture. From memory, write the text of the Great Commission. What church efforts fall under the Great Commission? Where do we suppose the Great Commission is accomplished? Who is responsible for accomplishing the Great Commission?

Common answers for Great Commission efforts are missionary work, evangelism training, and seeker services. We commonly think of Great Commission efforts happening "over there," usually in the 10/40 Window[33] or third-world countries. As a result, many Christians believe that the Great Commission is accomplished mostly by missionaries.

Why is this "missionary mandate" the common understanding? The reason again goes back to the 1600s.

The first reference to 'The Great Commission' is found in the writings of a Dutch missionary named Justinian von Welz (1621-88).[34] The common interpretation of his day was that the commission was given exclusively to the apostles. But the term 'Great Commission' wasn't popularized until Hudson Taylor used it in his effort to establish the China Inland Mission in the mid- to late-1800s.[35] Other researchers cite the father of modern missions, William Carey, as the turning point for the term's use for emphasizing that the Great Commission was the responsibility of every Christian and not a command isolated to the apostles.[36] The missions thrust of these post-Reformation leaders gave the Great Commission a decidedly evangelistic interpretation. And the reason the name became so popular may have resulted in the very reason the church has such a hard time accomplishing the mission.

Let's look at the text.

> Now the eleven disciples went to Galilee, to the mountain to which Jesus had directed them. 17 And when they saw him they worshiped him, but some doubted. 18 And Jesus came and said to them, "All authority in heaven and on earth has been given to me. 19 Go therefore and make disciples of all nations, baptizing them in the name of the Father and of the Son and of the Holy Spirit, 20 teaching them to observe all that I have commanded you. And behold, I am with you always, to the end of the age." (Matthew 28:16–20 ESV)

Colin Marshall and Tony Payne, authors of *The Trellis and the Vine*, note that our English translations lead us to believe that the main emphasis of the commission is to 'go.' "But the main verb of the sentence is 'make disciples', with three subordinate participles hanging off it: going (or 'as you go'), baptizing and teaching."[37]

The word 'nations' also leads us to think that the Great Commission is to be done "over there." But Dallas Willard points out that perhaps a better translation of "ἔθνη" in verse 19 is 'ethnic groups,' or 'people of every kind.' "But this leads in practice to not treating 'our kind of people' as the ones to be led into discipleship to Jesus. Some actually think that 'we' don't need it, because we are basically right to begin with. But in fact the primary mission field for the Great Commission today is made up of the churches in Europe and North America."[38]

The emphasis on missions has led us to believe that the Great Commission is about conversions. A modern condensed interpretation is, "Go get people saved!" But let's think about that. Are we really saying that God is expecting _us_ to save people? Do we really think that _we_ can bring people to a point of conviction? What does scripture say?

> Nevertheless, I tell you the truth: it is to your advantage that I go away, for if I do not go away, the Helper will not come to you. But if I go, I will send him to you. 8 And when he comes, _he will convict the world concerning sin and righteousness and judgment_: 9 concerning sin, because they do not believe in me; 10 concerning righteousness, because I go to the Father, and you will see me no longer; 11 concerning judgment, because the ruler of this world is judged. (John 16:7-11 ESV)

> 42 And they devoted themselves to the apostles' teaching and the fellowship, to the breaking of bread and the prayers. 43 And awe came upon every soul, and many wonders and signs were being done through the apostles. 44 And all who believed were together and had all things in common. 45 And they were selling their possessions and belongings and distributing the proceeds to all, as any had need. 46 And day by day, attending the temple together and breaking bread

in their homes, they received their food with glad and generous hearts, 47 praising God and having favor with all the people. <u>And the Lord added to their number day by day those who were being saved.</u> (Acts 2:42-47 ESV)

<u>And the hand of the Lord was with them</u>, and a great number who believed turned to the Lord. (Acts 11:21 ESV)

We know that it's <u>God</u> who saves people, and it's the <u>Holy Spirit</u> who convicts people of sin. Our job is to partner with God, so the question is what is our role in the partnership? Jesus tells us it is making disciples, teaching them to observe all he has commanded.

Why should our primary focus be on discipleship? Because if we keep trying to do what only God can do, and we ignore the task that we've been given, then the work of discipleship doesn't happen. The task of making disciples is a partnership. The Holy Spirit convicts people of sin; they are reconciled to God the Father through the sacrifice of Jesus his Son; and the church makes disciples of them, who then make disciples who make disciples.

Two more things before we begin our approach to a disciple-making church. First, what's another reason for Jesus to say, "of all nations" in Matt 28:19?

Because even after his ascension, the early church believed that this was a gospel message to the Jews exclusively. They were surprised when God began transforming Gentiles and adding them to the Kingdom of God (see Acts 10-15; especially Acts 10:34-48, and 15:12-35). The "of all nations" in effect meant "not just the children of Israel." It wasn't about overseas missions; it was about the Kingdom of God destroying the ethnic divisions and the religious pride of Jewish believers. He wants us to invite ALL people into the Kingdom of God!

Also, let's look at the Great Commission from Mark's point of view.

14 Afterward he appeared to the eleven themselves as they were reclining at table, and he rebuked them for their unbelief and hardness of heart, because they had not believed those who saw him after he had risen. 15 And he said to them, "Go into all the world and proclaim the gospel to the whole creation. 16 Whoever believes and is baptized will be saved, but whoever does not believe will be condemned. (Mark 16:14-16 ESV)

Why does Jesus say, "to the whole Creation" in verse 15? Why didn't he say, "to every person"? Because the gospel (good news) of the Kingdom of God is good news to all creation – not just humans (remember Romans 8:19-20). The fall made it impossible for men and women to fully realize humanity's role as kingdom stewards. We needed reconciliation not only to deal with humanity's sin problem; we also needed reconciliation to restore our identity as stewards of creation and representatives of God in the world. And the world knows we need more stewards of the Kingdom of God. We need more Representatives of God in the world. The Great Commission is how we get there.

354

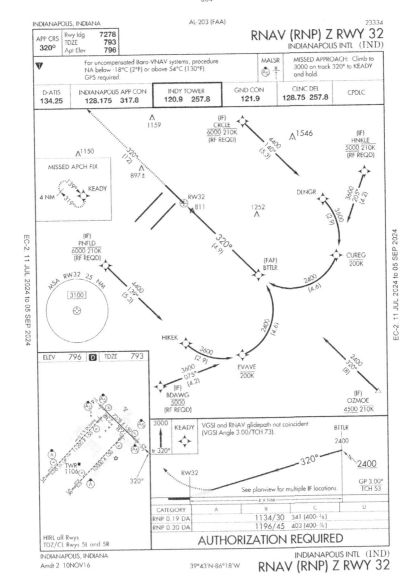

WAYPOINT 7 – THE PRACTICE OF THE KINGDOM OF GOD

*We Must See The Church Individually
As Well As Corporately*

Now we begin our final approach toward a disciple-making church. We have reached our final waypoint: The Church. Before we can grasp a vision for what a disciple-making church looks like, we need to answer the question, "What is the Church?" The answer to that question may require a final one-degree course adjustment.

If we don't understand what the church is (its identity), and we don't understand what ministry in the church is supposed to look like (its vision), we won't have a clue as to what strategies to implement to accomplish the mission.

The first thing we must determine is, is the church singular or plural? Do we see the church corporately or individually? The answer is both.

We must recognize that the church is both singular (there is one body – the church singular) and plural (each member of the body, as they exercise their gifts, is the church doing ministry – the church plural). Unfortunately, the Church usually sees itself corporately (singular) when thinking missionally, and individually (plural) when thinking about benefits. The common thought, whether we say it or not, is "the church (corporately) does the work, and the church (individually) goes to heaven when we die."

As a result, we have centralized ministry to the point that we assume that ministry only happens when the church is working together in an organized, programmed effort. The church tends to substitute programming in place of discipleship. And there's a good reason … programming is easier than discipleship. It takes less effort and can happen quicker. Discipleship is relational and takes place over several months or years. Programming can be delegated and culminates in an event.

There are other reasons why programming is easier than discipleship. Programming is measurable. Did the event happen or not? Was attendance what we expected or not? Did it result in decisions for Christ or not? And in some less-than-spiritual analysis, did we make money, or did we just break even?

Discipleship is harder to measure. Bobby Harrington is convinced that discipleship isn't just an eight-week Bible study but requires long-term relationships. "He [Jesus] showed us that the fundamental methodology in making disciples is relationships. Discipleship is the focus. Relationships are the method. Jesus invited people into relationships with himself; he loved them and, in the process, showed them how to follow God and become like him. His primary method was life-on-life."[39]

What could happen if we decentralized ministry? What could happen if the church started thinking of the church as *the church plural*; each member of the body, exercising their gifts daily, doing ministry in the circles they travel in? Programmed ministry is fine and effective, but it can't be the only tool in the ministry toolbox. I would argue that it shouldn't be the *primary* tool in the ministry toolbox. One-on-one ministry by the church plural should be the primary way that ministry happens in the Kingdom of God.

Why is it important to know and affirm that the church is both corporate (singular) and individual (plural)? Because familiar scriptures then take on a greater sense of urgency and call the church to respond.

Are we intentionally using scripture for teaching, reproof, correction, and training in righteousness for the specific purpose of making sure that every man and woman is equipped for every good work? (2 Timothy 3:14-17)

Do we operate in ways that affirm *not only* that we are saved by grace through faith, and not of works, *but also* that we affirm that every born-again man and woman are the craftsmanship of God, created in Christ Jesus for good works that God has already planned ahead of time for each of them to accomplish? (Ephesians 2:8-10)

Do we understand and operate in ways that affirm that the Lord Jesus equips each disciple with everything good so that we each can do his will, as it is in heaven, and that the Kingdom of God can advance? (Hebrews 13:20-21, Matthew 6:10)

Does the church function in ways that make it obvious we believe that God is able to make all grace abound to each disciple, not only to save us from sin, but to ensure that we are each sufficiently equipped in all things and at all times, to exceed in every good work that the Father has prepared for us? (2 Corinthians 9:8)

Twenty years ago, Dallas Willard lamented, "I know of no current denomination or local congregation that has a concrete plan and practice for teaching people to do 'all things whatsoever I have commanded you.' Very few even regard this as something we should actually try to do, and many think it to be simply impossible."[40]

Affirming that the church exists both corporately and individually, and that the primary tool in the church ministry toolbox should be the church plural, deployed for one-on-one ministry in their day-to-day lives, would go a long way toward accomplishing what some think to be "simply impossible."

It's time to store your onboard electrical devices and buckle up. We are about to arrive at our destination.

508

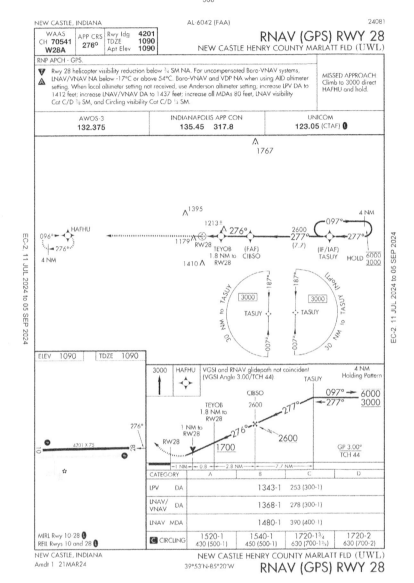

508
NEW CASTLE, INDIANA
AL-6042 (FAA)
24081
WAAS CH 70541 W28A
APP CRS 276°
Rwy ldg 4201
TDZE 1090
Apt Elev 1090
RNAV (GPS) RWY 28
NEW CASTLE HENRY COUNTY MARLATT FLD (UWL)
RNP APCH - GPS.
Rwy 28 helicopter visibility reduction below ¾ SM NA. For uncompensated Baro-VNAV systems, LNAV/VNAV NA below -17°C or above 54°C. Baro-VNAV and VDP NA when using AID altimeter setting. When local altimeter setting not received, use Anderson altimeter setting, increase LPV DA to 1412 feet; increase LNAV/VNAV DA to 1437 feet; increase all MDAs 80 feet, LNAV visibility Cat C/D ⅜ SM, and Circling visibility Cat C/D ¼ SM.
MISSED APPROACH: Climb to 3000 direct HAFHU and hold.
AWOS-3 132.375
INDIANAPOLIS APP CON 135.45 317.8
UNICOM 123.05 (CTAF)
1767
1395
1213±
276°
2600
277°
(7.7)
097°
4 NM
277°
HAFHU
096°
276°
4 NM
1179
RW28
TEYOB 1.8 NM to RW28
(FAF) CIBSO
(IF/IAF) TASUY
HOLD 6000 3000
1410
187°
007°
3000
TASUY
30 NM to TASUY
(NoPT)
EC-2, 11 JUL 2024 to 05 SEP 2024
ELEV 1090
TDZE 1090
276°
4201 X 75
10
28
MIRL Rwy 10-28
REIL Rwys 10 and 28
3000
HAFHU
VGSI and RNAV glidepath not coincident (VGSI Angle 3.00/TCH 44)
4 NM Holding Pattern
TASUY
CIBSO 2600
TEYOB 1.8 NM to RW28
1 NM to RW28
RW28
1700
2600
097° 6000
277° 3000
GP 3.00° TCH 44
1 NM 0.8 2.8 NM 7.7 NM
CATEGORY A B C D
LPV DA 1343-1 253 (300-1)
LNAV/VNAV DA 1368-1 278 (300-1)
LNAV MDA 1480-1 390 (400-1)
CIRCLING 1520-1 430 (500-1) 1540-1 450 (500-1) 1720-1¾ 630 (700-1¾) 1720-2 630 (700-2)
NEW CASTLE, INDIANA
Amdt 1 21MAR24
39°53'N-85°20'W
NEW CASTLE HENRY COUNTY MARLATT FLD (UWL)
RNAV (GPS) RWY 28

CONCLUSION – A VISION OF DISCIPLESHIP IN THE KINGDOM OF GOD

I f you've stayed with us through the entire trip, you'll recall that we've made seven one-degree course corrections at seven different waypoints. Our compass of "seeking first the Kingdom of God" has guided us through each adjustment.

Viewing the world through the metanarrative of scripture, we've seen that God's good creation was the initiation of the Kingdom of God, and even after the fall in the garden, God promised to make all things new. We discovered that God created every human being to be stewards of his creation, and his representatives in the world.

At the third waypoint we saw the need to expand our view of the gospel, and that the good news was that the Kingdom of God was at hand and was advancing due to Christ's sacrifice on the cross and the resurrection that validated his rule and authority. We examined salvation and saw that it was necessary not only to solve the sin problem, but to restore men and women to their role as stewards of creation and representatives of God.

Passing through the fifth waypoint, we saw discipleship is not about "preparing believers for heaven" but equipping disciples to be successful in accomplishing their role as God's stewards and representatives. We adjusted our perspective on the Great Commission as an every-person, everyday mission, and not just sending missionaries to the 10/40 window.

As we began our final approach to a disciple-making church, we saw that the church exists both corporately (the church singular) and individually (the church plural), and that while ministry happens in both realms, the primary tool in the church's toolbox should be one-on-one ministry in the day-to-day lives of every disciple.

By applying these course corrections, we can establish a theological foundation that upholds the goodness of God's creation and our responsibility to steward it. We believe that men and women have been called to represent God in the world and that Jesus and his disciples preached the good news of the present reality of the Kingdom of God. Through Christ's sacrifice on the cross, we have been redeemed from sin and restored to our role as stewards of the Kingdom of God. Therefore, we affirm that discipleship is essential in equipping every believer to faithfully steward God's creation, and the Great Commission applies to every Christian in every aspect of their daily lives. Lastly, we believe that the church functions as a united body, as well as individually through its members, who partner with the Holy Spirit daily to advance the Kingdom of God.

The cabin doors are now open, and you are free to disembark. But let me highlight some of the things you will see in the New

Country of Discipleship in the Kingdom of God that will require further investigation.

The first thing that catches your eye might be that gift-based ministry will overshadow program-based ministry. You will still see program-based ministry, but only for efforts that require the entire church body to accomplish. This will be where young disciples will discover most of their ministry opportunities, but they will be encouraged by their disciple-makers to discover how they can be stewards of the Kingdom of God in their daily lives and take ministry outside the walls of the church building.

Conversations in the new country will center more around what people have been saved FOR and less about what people have been saved FROM. Disciples will talk about how God has been working through their lives, and how they have seen him working in their friends and family. They will share how the Holy Spirit has prompted them to say or do something, and how that partnership has been fruitful in advancing the Kingdom of God.

Discipleship efforts in the new country will not be primarily short-term Bible study efforts that only transfer knowledge. Disciples will be challenged to grow in one-on-one relationships that will encourage cognitive growth (what they know), but also will encourage and expect to see affective (their emotions, passions, and desires) and behavioral (how they act and react, their habits) growth.[41] Discipleship is messy. There are seasons of growth followed by seasons of pruning. Some seasons burst forth with rapid change, and others are seasons of rest. But disciple makers are reminded that God is the Lord of the Harvest.

You will notice a reduced desire for cookie-cutter program solutions. The church has learned that a program that works in one church or region may not work in another one. A program that works during a particular season (or for a particular generation) may not work in the future. As they work on developing ministry ideas that work in their location, in their particular season, for a specific generation, they avoid the danger of developing systematic discipleship activities that drift into focusing on the program at the expense of the students.[42] The goal of any program must always be the spiritual growth and maturity of each disciple.

Senior pastors are spending less time on administrative tasks like attending meetings and making decisions regarding church property and programs, while spending more time on intentional, long-term, discipleship relationships with a handful of leaders, who will then replicate the discipleship process in others.[43]

These senior pastors have embraced disciple-making as the core mission of the local church. Their churches and personal ministries have shifted to focus on Jesus-style disciple-making.[44]

You might notice that there is a clear consensus and understanding of discipleship-language that reflects a biblical perspective on terms like discipleship, the Great Commission, the gospel, and salvation, and this commonly understood language is taught consistently and continually through all generations.[45]

When church leaders in the new country make decisions on how to spend their resources, every decision passes through the same filter: "How does this help us make disciples who make disciples?"[46]

You'll be excited when you discover that there is literally a Bible-reading movement in families, churches, neighborhoods, workplaces, sports leagues, and schools. It's a normal part of everyday life where believers are reading the Bible with their children before bed, with their spouse over breakfast, with a non-Christian colleague at work over lunch, with the person they are discipling, and with the one that is discipling them.[47]

You will notice a significant change in the way Christians usually invite people to become part of the Kingdom of God. The old invitation was: "God loves you and has a wonderful plan for your life. Accept Christ and one day you will escape earth and live forever in heaven. These are all the benefits of following Christ. Come join us at church." The new invitation is: "God loves this messed up world we live in. He sees the pain, and injustice, the broken-hearted, and he wants you to help transform the world. God is in the business of re-creation; of taking what's broken and making it new (not just *like new*). Come help us change the world!" This appeal resonates well with Postmoderns, Metamoderns, Gen Z, and Generation Alpha who are concerned about righting wrongs, correcting injustice, eliminating establishment chaos – all the things that exist in the world that they were designed to steward.

You might even notice a slower pace from conversion to baptism. Discipleship has become a serious matter. Ministers have pondered serious questions in the new country like, "Do we have authority to baptize people who have not been brought to a clear decision to be a disciple of Christ? Do we encourage 'believers' who refuse discipleship, that they are at peace with God and God is at peace with them?"[48]

As you explore the new country, you discover a monument with a plaque inscribed with a quote from Dallas Willard. It is a challenge that helped transform and rebirth the new country. As such, it is given a place of great honor, but also serves to continually remind the residents what is required to keep the new country a living example of discipleship in the Kingdom of God.

The greatest issue facing the world today, with all its heartbreaking needs, is whether those who, by profession or culture, are identified as 'Christians' will become disciples – students, apprentices, practitioners – of Jesus Christ, steadily learning from him how to live the life of the Kingdom of the Heavens into every corner of human existence. Will they break out of the churches to be his Church – to be, without human force or violence, his mighty force for good on earth, drawing the churches after them toward the eternal purposes of God?... There is no greater issue facing the individual human being, Christian or not.[49]

[1] Grey Matter Research & Consulting and Discipleship.org, "National Study on Disciple Making in USA Churches: High Aspirations Amidst Disappointing Results (PDF)" (Grey Matter Research & Consulting, March 2020), 3.

[2] Grey Matter Research & Consulting and Discipleship.org, 8.

[3] Grey Matter Research & Consulting and Discipleship.org, 6.

[4] Dallas Willard, *The Great Omission: Reclaiming Jesus's Essential Teachings on Discipleship*, First Edition (San Francisco, CA: HarperOne, 2006), 4.

[5] Willard, 69.

[6] Willard, xi.

[7] Walter A. Elwell, ed., *Baker Encyclopedia of the Bible, Volumes 1 and 2* (Grand Rapids, MI: Baker Pub Group, 1988), 539.

[8] N. T. Wright, "Resurrection of the Dead," in *Dictionary for Theological Interpretation of the Bible* (London: Grand Rapids, MI: Baker Academic, November 1, 2005), 676–77.

[9] Joseph A. Jr. Pipa et al., *TH331 Perspectives on Creation: Five Views on Its Meaning and Significance (5 Hour Course)*, Logos Mobile Education (Bellingham, WA: Lexham Press, 2017), sec. 1.

[10] Pipa et al., sec. 9.

[11] Pipa et al., sec. 21.

[12] Pipa et al., sec. 30.

[13] Pipa et al., sec. 37.

[14] Bill Hull and Ben Sobels, *The Discipleship Gospel: What Jesus Preached—We Must Follow* (HIM Publications, 2018), 9.

[15] Hull and Sobels, 17.

[16] Hull and Sobels, 23.

[17] Hull and Sobels, 29.

[18] Scot McKnight, Dallas Willard, and N. T. Wright, *The King Jesus Gospel: The Original Good News Revisited*, Logos Reader Edition (Grand Rapids, MI: Zondervan, 2016), 12.

[19] Dallas Willard, *The Divine Conspiracy: Rediscovering Our Hidden Life In God*, 1st edition (San Francisco, CA: Harper, 1998), 403.

[20] Willard, *The Great Omission*, 13.

[21] Hull and Sobels, *The Discipleship Gospel*, 10.

[22] David F. Wright, Sinclair B. Ferguson, and J. I. Packer, eds., *New Dictionary of Theology*, First Edition first Printing (Downers Grove, IL: IVP Academic, 1988), 592.

[23] Frank A. James (III), *CH102 Introducing Church History II: Reformation to Postmodernism (7 Hour Course)* (Bellingham, WA: Lexham Press, 2016), sec. 37.

[24] Rick Brannan, *Creeds, Confessions, and Catechisms: A Guide*, Logos Research Edition (Bellingham, WA: Faithlife, 2021), art. The Westminster Shorter Catechism.

[25] Philip Schaff, *The Creeds of Christendom, with a History and Critical Notes: The Evangelical Protestant Creeds, with Translations*, Logos Research Edition, vol. 3, The Creeds of Christendom (New York: Harper & Brothers, 1882), 676.

[26] Frederick Cardoza and Thom Blair, *ED205 Discipleship in History and Practice*, Logos Research Edition (Bellingham, WA: Lexham Press, 2016), sec. 38.

[27] Michael J. Anthony et al., eds., *Evangelical Dictionary of Christian Education*, Logos Research Edition (Grand Rapids, MI: Baker Academic, 2001), 441.

[28] Bobby Harrington and Alex Absalom, *Discipleship That Fits: An eBook That Introduces the 5 Disciple Making Contexts (PDF)* (Discipleship.org, 2016), 15.

[29] Harrington and Absalom, 22.

[30] Bobby Harrington, *Discipleship Is the Core Mission of the Church: Helping People Trust and Follow Jesus (PDF)*, 1st edition (Exponential, 2014), 32.

[31] Jim Putman, *Real-Life Discipleship: Building Churches That Make Disciples*, Logos Research Edition (Colorado Springs, CO: NavPress, 2010), 20.

[32] Willard, *The Great Omission*, 104.

[33] The 10/40 Window is a section of the earth north of the equator running from 10 degrees north to 40 degrees north longitude. It encompasses North Africa, the Middle East, and Asia and contains two-thirds of the world's population about 5.33 billion people. According to the Joshua Project, this includes nearly 9,000 distinct people groups, two-thirds of which are considered unreached with the Gospel of the Kingdom of God. "10/40 Window," Joshua Project, accessed February 23, 2024, https://joshuaproject.net/resources/articles/10_40_window

[34] Robbie F. Castlemann, "The Last Word: The Great Commission: Ecclesiology," *Themelios* 32, no. 3 (2007): 68.

[35] F. L. Cross and Elizabeth A. Livingstone, eds., *The Oxford Dictionary of the Christian Church*, Logos Research Edition (Oxford; New York: Oxford University Press, 2005), 1591.

[36] Colin Marshall and Tony Payne, *The Trellis and the Vine*, 2nd edition (Matthias Media, 2021), 11.

[37] Marshall and Payne, 12.

[38] Willard, *The Great Omission*, xiii.

[39] Harrington, *Discipleship Is the Core Mission of the Church*, 13.

[40] Willard, *The Great Omission*, 72–73.

[41] Cardoza and Blair, *ED205*, sec. 55.

[42] Cardoza and Blair, sec. 82.

[43] Marshall and Payne, *The Trellis and the Vine*, 25–26.

[44] Grey Matter Research & Consulting and Discipleship.org, "Disciple Making Study," 4.

[45] Grey Matter Research & Consulting and Discipleship.org, 15.

[46] Grey Matter Research & Consulting and Discipleship.org, 13.

[47] Marshall and Payne, *The Trellis and the Vine*, 57.

[48] Willard, *The Great Omission*, 11.

[49] Willard, xv.

AFTER YOU READ
THIS BOOK

In the space below and on the next page, answer these questions *AFTER YOU READ THIS BOOK*:

1. What is the Great Commission?

2. What is discipleship?

3. How do you determine whether ministry is effective?

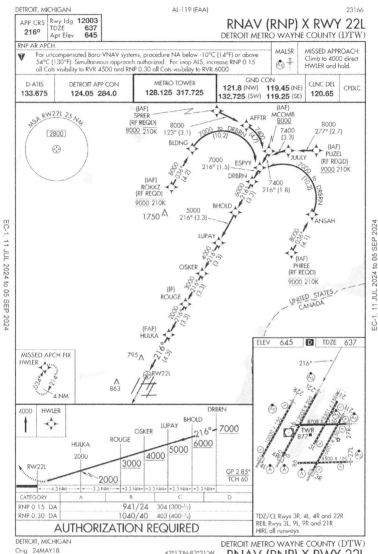

DISCUSSION QUESTIONS

The Problem

1. List three efforts in your ministry that focus on discipleing believers.

2. Do you agree with the Dallas Willard quote that one "is not required to be … a disciple in order to become a Christian, and one may remain a Christian without any signs of progress toward, or in, discipleship?" If so, how do we change the status quo?

3. How do you read Matthew 6:33? What does it mean to "seek first the kingdom of God?" How would you rephrase it? Does it mean:
   a. Before seeking anything else, make sure you seek God first.
   b. Make it a priority in your life to always seek the kingdom of God.
   c. Be observant and find the places in your community where the kingdom of God exists.
   d. Something else …

Waypoint 1 – The Metanarrative – Creation and the Kingdom of God

1. Do you believe that there is one overarching story in the Bible from Genesis to Revelation? If so, what is it?

2. Do you believe that the Old Testament story is different from the New Testament story? If so, how are they different?

3. Some people think that the "fall" in the garden caused God to change his plans, while others say that God planned for there to be a "fall" in the garden. What do you think?

4. Do you believe that the created world is "good," "broken but fixable," "irredeemably broken," or would you describe it some other way?

Waypoint 2 – The Role of Humanity – Stewards of the Kingdom of God

1. How does being a steward of creation differ from being a priest representing God to the world? Are there similarities in those roles?

2. In what ways does God "give us the kingdom?" (Luke 12:32)

3. If God designed creation in such a way that it requires intervention (either by God or humans), how does that change your view of God?

4. If God created a world that requires intervention, doesn't that imply that created an imperfect world? Or does it imply that all of creation is similar to children, who require daily intervention and connection with others as they grow and mature?

Waypoint 3 – The Good News – The Gospel of the Kingdom of God vs. Other Gospels

1. If Jesus and his disciples were preaching the gospel (good news) before his death and resurrection, does that mean that their efforts were incomplete or ineffective?

2. Describe the difference between the gospel of salvation and the gospel of the kingdom of God, if any.

3. Have you seen examples of ministers of Christ preaching other gospels (i.e., left, right, prosperity, consumer, etc.)? If so, how do we ensure that we are proclaiming the full gospel of the kingdom of God?

4. Do you believe someone can accept Jesus as Savior but not submit to him as Lord? Why or why not?

Waypoint 4 – The Mission of Christ – The Reconciliation of the Stewards of the Kingdom of God

1. In Colossians 1:15-23, what do you think it means that through Christ God was reconciling "to himself all things?" What is included in "all things?"

2. Do you agree that all of Creation needs to be reconciled to God as well as all humans? Why or why not?

3. Do you agree that the commission given in Genesis 1:26-28 is still applicable to men and women today?

4. The disciples believed that the resurrection of Christ was the beginning of God making "all things new." What are some things in your life or community that need to be "made new" by the power of God?

Waypoint 5 – The Missing Piece – The Restoration of the Stewards of the Kingdom of God

1. Have you ever seen an example of healthy discipleship in your experience? What should be included in a healthy discipleship process?

2. The author makes the argument that "the chief end of man" is to fear God and obey his commands. Tradition tells us that "the chief end of man" is to glorify God and enjoy him forever. What would you describe as being the chief end of man? Give reasons to support your position.

3. For men and women without children, how should they seek to live out the Shema found in Deuteronomy 6:4-7?

4. If discipleship is both "learning the playbook AND running the drills," how should our practice of discipleship change? What would a "discipleing apprenticeship" look like?

Waypoint 6 – The Commission – The Mission of the Stewards of the Kingdom of God

1. If the primary verb in the Great Commission is "make disciples," and the secondary actions are "as you go," baptizing, and teaching, how should that impact our discipleship efforts?

2. If discipleship is what happens after someone is saved, how does that impact our discipleship efforts?

3. We've seen in the last few chapters that Christ's sacrifice on the cross not only resolved our sin problem but also restored our identity as representatives of God and stewards of his creation. This indicates that action on the part of the disciples is required. Can you identify three things that you could do to accomplish the commission of making disciples in your community?

Waypoint 7 – The Church – The Practice of the Kingdom of God

1. Would you describe your congregation as more singular (the church acts as a whole), or more plural (the individual members act individually)? Is that a good thing, or should there be some adjustments?

2. In your congregation has programming been substituted for discipleship? Are there some programs in the church that should die? If so, how could you refocus your resources to replace the program with discipleship?

3. In your church context, can you think of at least two ways you could accurately measure intentional, effective discipleship? What metrics would determine how effective your congregation is at intentional, effective discipleship?

The New Country – A Vision of Discipleship in the Kingdom of God

1. Can you identify the top three waypoints where a course correction would benefit your local church?

2. Have you had a conversation with a fellow believer about what you think you've been saved FOR? What do you feel God might be calling you to do based on your gifts and passions?

3. How can you improve your accountability for reading and studying

scripture? Could you join or start a bible study that dives deep into scripture?

4. How do you measure maturity in a disciple? What metrics could you use to determine if someone is growing in their faith?

5. Are there leaders in your congregation that can partner with your pastor to take on his or her responsibilities, and enable your pastor to intentionally disciple other believers?

6. What would it take to transform your congregation's "elevator pitch" to your community from "Come join our church!" to "Come help us change the world!"

<u>NOTES</u>

BIBLIOGRAPHY

Anthony, Michael J., Warren S. Benson, Daryl Eldridge, and Julie Gorman, eds. *Evangelical Dictionary of Christian Education.* Logos Research Edition. Grand Rapids, MI: Baker Academic, 2001.

Brannan, Rick. *Creeds, Confessions, and Catechisms: A Guide.* Logos Research Edition. Bellingham, WA: Faithlife, 2021.

Cardoza, Frederick, and Thom Blair. *ED205 Discipleship in History and Practice.* Logos Research Edition. Bellingham, WA: Lexham Press, 2016.

Castlemann, Robbie F. "The Last Word: The Great Commission: Ecclesiology." *Themelios* 32, no. 3 (2007): 68–70.

Cross, F. L., and Elizabeth A. Livingstone, eds. *The Oxford Dictionary of the Christian Church.* Logos Research Edition. Oxford; New York: Oxford University Press, 2005.

Elwell, Walter A., ed. *Baker Encyclopedia of the Bible, Volumes 1 and 2.* Grand Rapids, MI: Baker Pub Group, 1988.

Gary Matter Research & Consulting and Discipleship.org. "National Study on Disciple Making in USA Churches: High Aspirations Amidst Disappointing Results (PDF)." Grey Matter Research & Consulting, March 2020.

Harrington, Bobby. *Discipleship Is the Core Mission of the Church: Helping People Trust and Follow Jesus (PDF).* 1st edition. Exponential, 2014.

Harrington, Bobby, and Alex Absalom. *Discipleship That Fits: An eBook That Introduces the 5 Disciple Making Contexts (PDF)*. Discipleship.org, 2016.

Hull, Bill, and Ben Sobels. *The Discipleship Gospel: What Jesus Preached—We Must Follow*. HIM Publications, 2018.

James, Frank A., (III). *CH102 Introducing Church History II: Reformation to Postmodernism (7 Hour Course)*. Bellingham, WA: Lexham Press, 2016.

Joshua Project. "10/40 Window | Joshua Project." Accessed February 23, 2024. https://joshuaproject.net/resources/articles/10_40_window.

Marshall, Colin, and Tony Payne. *The Trellis and the Vine*. 2nd edition. Matthias Media, 2021.

McKnight, Scot, Dallas Willard, and N. T. Wright. *The King Jesus Gospel: The Original Good News Revisited*. Logos Reader Edition. Grand Rapids, MI: Zondervan, 2016.

Pipa, Joseph A. Jr., Mark D. Futato, C. John Collins, Tremper Longman III, and John H. Walton. *TH331 Perspectives on Creation: Five Views on Its Meaning and Significance (5 Hour Course)*. Logos Mobile Education. Bellingham, WA: Lexham Press, 2017.

Putman, Jim. *Real-Life Discipleship: Building Churches That Make Disciples*. Logos Research Edition. Colorado Springs, CO: NavPress, 2010.

Schaff, Philip. *The Creeds of Christendom, with a History and Critical Notes: The Evangelical Protestant Creeds, with Translations*. Logos Research Edition. Vol. 3. 3 vols. The Creeds of Christendom. New York: Harper & Brothers, 1882.

Willard, Dallas. *The Divine Conspiracy: Rediscovering Our Hidden Life In God*. 1st edition. San Francisco, CA: Harper, 1998.

———. *The Great Omission: Reclaiming Jesus's Essential Teachings on Discipleship*. First Edition. San Francisco, CA: HarperOne, 2006.

Wright, David F., Sinclair B. Ferguson, and J. I. Packer, eds. *New Dictionary of Theology*. First Edition first Printing. Downers Grove, IL: IVP Academic, 1988.

Wright, N. T. "Resurrection of the Dead." In *Dictionary for Theological Interpretation of the Bible*, 676–78. London: Grand Rapids, MI: Baker Academic, November 1, 2005.

ACKNOWLEDGEMENTS

I could not have completed my degree or this project without the encouragement and support of my wife Cheryl. She has helped carry the load these past few years as I pursued my training and completed this guide. She is a gift from God and my partner in ministry forever.

Over the past several years I have been challenged, encouraged, and supported by Rev. Jeannette Flynn. Jeannette and I have sharpened each other "as iron sharpens iron" as we served on ministry teams together in the Church of God (Anderson, IN), as campmeeting evangelists, and in pastoral ministry. She has influenced my ministry in so many ways and it has been a joy to serve alongside her.

Rev. Dr. Jerry D. Ingalls is my pastor, brother in Christ, and kindred spirit. It seems that the Spirit of God has been speaking the same word to each of us over the last few years, and that word has frequently focused on discipleship. I am indebted to him for introducing me to the writings of Dr. Michael S. Heiser and N.T. Wright. I pray that we will see many future harvest seasons as a result of our time together in Henry County, Indiana.

Thanks to IN State Representative Mike Speedy, and my nephew Isaac Ferrell for clarifying the navigation terminology that became the motif for this leadership guide. The imagery of aviation waypoints gave me a framework to communicate what God was stirring in my spirit.

Many thanks go to First Baptist Church in New Castle, IN for encouraging and supporting Cheryl and me as we followed the call to serve as interim worship leaders in a neighboring congregation and considering us missionaries being sent to the larger body of Christ. Thanks also go to South Memorial Drive Church of God in New Castle, IN who welcomed us to Indiana more than two decades ago and supported us in seasons of blessing and seasons of trial. These two congregations also served as my focus group, whose involvement helped polish the rough ideas that seeded this guide.

To Dr. Michael S. Heiser I am forever indebted. Though we never met face-to-face, I consider him a mentor and long-distance professor. His writings, including *The Unseen Realm: Recovering the Supernatural Worldview of the Bible*, his *Naked Bible Podcast*, and his AWKNG School of Theology, transformed the way I approach and read Scripture, and set me on a course to complete my degree at Redemption Seminary.

This book would never have happened in this configuration if not for Redemption Seminary and my Professor-Mentors: Dr. John Raymond; Dr. Michael Collender, Ph.D.; Dr. Alexandria Ford; Dr. Coleman M. Ford, Ph.D.; Dr. Tom Sweeney; and Dr. Dale A. Bruggemann, Ph.D. Thank you for accepting me into the Master's Degree Program, and for the many hours of instruction and hard work you've invested in blazing a new trail in seminary education.

Finally, to God, in the lyrics of Andraé Crouch's *My Tribute*,
> How can I say thanks,
> For the things you have done for me?
> Things so undeserved,
> Yet you gave to prove your love for me.
> The voices of a million angels
> Could not express my gratitude.
> All that I am, and ever hope to be,
> I owe it all to Thee![1]

ABOUT THE AUTHOR

Curtis L. Ferrell

Curt Ferrell is currently working for the Indiana Department of Correction (IDOC) where he supervises a residential, evidence-based cognitive behavioral change program that focuses on faith and character. Additionally, he teaches biblical discipleship and leads worship in multiple settings.

Curt has a Master of Arts in Biblical Studies from Redemption Seminary and has been a lifelong student of Biblical and American history. He is passionate about encouraging Christians to assume their roles as stewards of the Kingdom of God and representatives of God in the world.

Curt has written adult and youth curriculum for the church including a group bible study called "Dual Citizenship: Living as A Christian In America," which has been published by Warner Press. He has authored more than sixty newspaper articles and has led worship workshops in Colorado, Indiana, Michigan, Tennessee, Wisconsin, and Indonesia. Curt is also a member of the American Society of Composers, Authors, and Publishers (ASCAP), and has helped produce four worship CD/Songbook projects.

Curt is an ordained minister in the Church of God (Anderson, IN) and has served as a pastor in churches located in Michigan and Indiana.

Curt and Cheryl have two adult daughters. One is an ordained pastor, and the other is a married elementary school teacher who also serves in children's ministry at a local church.

Curt Ferrell was born in Southwestern Ohio and grew up in Southwestern Michigan. He has lived and worked in Florida, Indiana, Michigan, and Ohio.

BOOKS BY THIS AUTHOR

Dual Citizenship: Living As A Christian In America

This six-week Bible study offers engaging discussion prompts, Scripture, and lessons on a Christian's role as citizens of both heaven and the United States as they wrestle with new ideas about how to approach civic and political engagement. Learners will come to know not only what the Bible teaches about our position with those in government and our eternal perspective, but also will experience the beauty of Christian community as they tackle this difficult topic. Appropriate for any youth through adult small group setting.

DUAL CITIZENSHIP

LIVING AS A CHRISTIAN IN AMERICA

GROUP BIBLE STUDY

Made in the USA
Columbia, SC
26 August 2024

41187657R00065